HOW TO
KEEP YOUR
SEX LIFE
ALIVE

HOW TO KEEP YOUR SEX LIFE ALIVE

ROBERT CHONIA

ATHENA PRESS
LONDON

First published 2009 by
ATHENA PRESS
Queen's House, 2 Holly Road
Twickenham TW1 4EG
United Kingdom

Printed for Athena Press

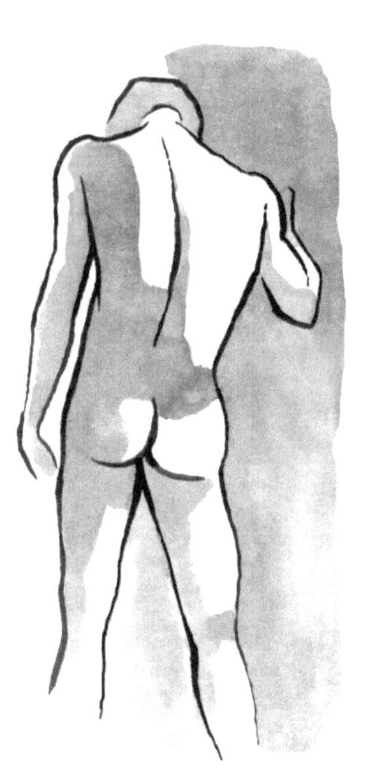

Preface

This book is meant for couples who find their sexual interest gradually fading away due to many years of sharing the same partner, or due to a lack of ideas on how to make the act interesting. Sexual activities are often practised behind closed doors and very little useful information is out there for people who would like to know more about it.

I believe that some of my experiences could be useful for those attempting to build a healthy relationship. In order to be true to the facts, I have written free of moral or religious restrictions. I expect readers, who I hope to be over the age of twenty, to be their own judges as to what is acceptable to them. One may not agree with some of my ideas but I think it's worth knowing what works for others.

Bear in mind that people are different. One man's meat might be another man's poison, so it's good to consider with caution what is good in a given situation. You may find nothing new or exciting as you read this, in which case I urge you to hand it over to someone else who may find it more useful.

Contents

Sexual Activities

Many people get very uncomfortable when it comes to talking about their sexual lives. I believe adults, who enjoy sex, must have room for talking about what it's all about. Most partners spend years together without discovering each other's sexual needs or desires. This is due to fear or lack of trust between them.

Before a couple can fully enjoy sex, they first have to overcome mistrust. Men and women often have fantasies that they keep to themselves. Some may expose a little of these fantasies under special conditions such as under the influence of alcohol, drugs or on a one-night stand with a secret lover or prostitute. It would be easier to share our fantasies with our partners if we could be open-minded about each other's desires. This, in effect, could help couples keep their partners and not risk losing them to prostitutes and other sex experts out there. It's a known fact that men especially go to whorehouses in order to live out their fantasies. There are sex experts out there who seem to know about people's desires to live their fantasies – and they are there to let them do just that. Your partner could be on a business trip and an encounter with such an expert could become a threat to your relationship because he or she will never be the same. Society puts fear into most of us and this fear can make our lives miserable. I think this should not be the case. Imagine your partner gives you all you need. Imagine having that angel and that devil in one packet. Studies show that partners who share so-called secret fantasies become bonded and stick together for a longer time.

Sexual Fantasies

∘ ○○ ◯ ○○ ∘

Sexual fantasies are stimulants for your sexual life and should not be overlooked. Sharing rich sexual fantasies with your partner can greatly enhance your sex life. However, some fantasies may be hard to fulfil in real life – some people may find the fantasies of others completely unacceptable or even physically impossible. Women's fantasies often differ from those of men. Some women fantasise about being raped or making love to a stranger in an unknown destination, where they won't be judged. Some fantasise about being strippers or prostitutes, or indulging in group sex. Even if some of these fantasies, although erotic, are not easy to fulfil in real life, it's good to work with the information and derive some interesting points from it.

I once had a friend, Ricky, whose girlfriend wanted to have sex with two guys – this had been her fantasy for years. Having spoken to some of my female friends, this seems to be a fantasy that many women have. She had feared to talk about it in her previous relationships but when she met Ricky she felt comfortable enough to tell him. She did not want to have sex with anyone they knew so, as the idea was equally exciting to Ricky, they worked with the information they had until they found a solution that satisfied both. He went shopping for a dildo – one that felt as near to the real thing as possible – blindfolded her and tickled her to get her ready for her fantasy. She was pleased with the dildo solution, and even though it was not the real thing she felt close enough to her fantasy and was therefore satisfied. The dildo became an active instrument in their sexual acts from then on.

Watching Penetration

A lot of men get turned on by watching erotic movies, while I have found, in researching this chapter, that women prefer not to. Well, there are a few things that come to my mind with regards to this issue. It's a great stimulant to watch how the sex organs interact when having sex. If you've never watched penetration, I strongly recommend it for both partners. Look at every stroke and admire how beautiful it is. The most ideal place to have sex is in a room with mirrors on the walls.

There are a lot of women who indulge in sexual activity but have never had a good look at the male organs and never seen how it shoots out sperm. The same applies to many men. Nature created a man different from a woman and it is exciting to observe the differences. This includes the differences in the structure of our bodies: the breasts, texture of skin, pubic hair, hands, feet, body smell and many more. It is often a great turn-on for women to see the sperm of a man and to feel it or even taste it.

Dirty Talk

Both men and women get highly stimulated with a certain degree of dirty talk. It seems like a little dark side of all humans that wants out and, once allowed, brings a strong bond and sense of closeness to a relationship.

Once again a couple should be able to find out what works for them. I once had a partner who would praise my erection. She would say things like, 'Fuck me hard… oh you are good… Yes, keep it right there… don't move… hit me… touch my breast… Oh, God, you are so strong… Oh I'm about to come… yeah it's coming…' While some may think this is wrong or vulgar, I find it very stimulating. This kind of talk was more than any aphrodisiac or Viagra to me and we both knew it.

I would also say things like, 'You like it eh? Take it… it's all yours, baby… open up wide… do you feel me? Take it all… Oh I feel you deep inside…' At times, through this kind of communication, we are able to reach orgasm at the same time. Dirty talk can be a great stimulant in sex acts. Imagine being in a public place and your partner suddenly whispering in your ear, 'I feel like making love to you right now.' This kind of dirty talk sends a high current through a man's body and can trigger great stimulation.

Dirty talk must be practised in the right environment however; you would not want your kids or neighbours to hear you. Whisper where necessary!

Equal Rights

It has almost become the norm in society that the male is expected to initiate the sexual act. Most women seem to fear initiating sex or even showing their male partners that they are interested. I think this is unfair. The fact is, most men like it when the female initiates the act, and since both men and women dislike rejection after making such an effort, care must be taken when one partner does not feel ready for the act. Equal rights must be exercised and rejections be polite and sensitive.

Foreplay

Foreplay is an act performed before intercourse in order to warm both parties up. It is important to have your partner ready for any sex act. Men are different from women when it comes to readiness for sex. A man can mentally prepare his body, have an erection and get close to ejaculation even before the act begins – especially on first dates. This can be very frustrating and disappointing for a woman with great expectations and can often be misinterpreted as weakness. I would rather say it is simply overexcitement.

It's good to spend time on foreplay. Kissing the lips and the neck area, sucking gently on the nipples, kissing the erotic zones and gently touching your partner's sexual organs can warm them up for the act. With practice and communication one can discover the sensitive areas of a partner, since this differs from person to person. A hard dick is a male sign of readiness, while a moist pussy is a female sign. Some women get moist when their feet are gently massaged and kissed, or when the back of their neck is kissed and gently bitten, or when warm air from the mouth hits the ear. There is so much to discover when it comes to this topic. Most men like it when their organs are gently held and kissed or the buttocks rubbed.

It can be very uncomfortable for a woman when insertion is forced under dry conditions. When the female is less moist, gel may be applied to avoid unwanted friction.

Massage

Massage is one act that relaxes the body. Occasionally massaging your partner with oil or body lotion can be equally fulfilling for you. It can also be a form of foreplay.

When certain areas of the body are gently massaged it can be very stimulating. Women love it when their buttocks are rubbed in oil. Another sensitive part is the anus area. Gently but firmly press your palm against the anus after rubbing the area in oil. Or mould your fingers into a ring and place it at the opening and gently press in and out. This, when done properly, can lead to orgasm. Rubbing a woman's feet, legs and thighs in oil can also be very exciting.

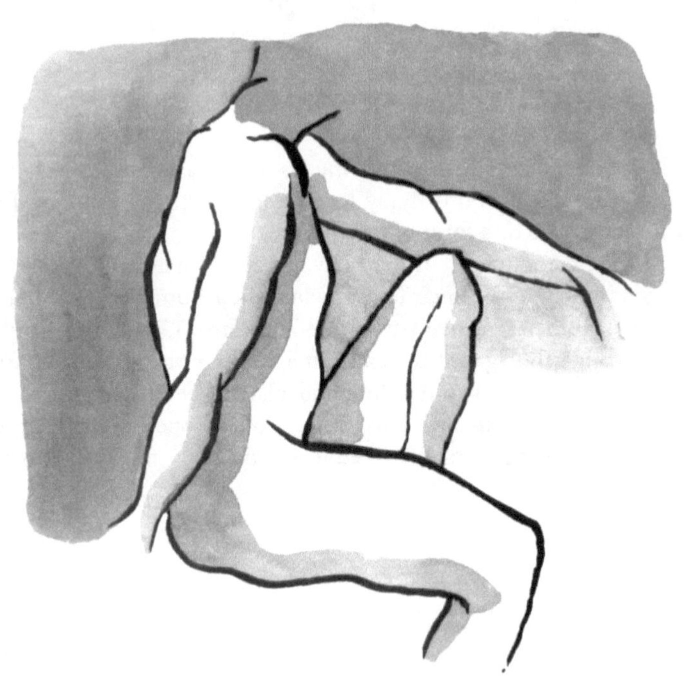

Masturbation

Masturbation is an act where each partner helps themselves to orgasm. This is usually achieved by using one's hands or by the help of dildos. Masturbation is another practice that people shy away from or prefer not to talk about even though both men and women indulge in it secretly. Many people like to do it in the bath or in the shower. With regards to female masturbation, the female places her fingers on her clitoris and rubs it into ecstasy. The male can learn how to stimulate the female partner by watching her do it all by herself.

For male masturbation, the male takes his penis in his hand and moves it up and down until it shoots out sperm. The female can also learn how best to bring the male to orgasm by watching. This act can be perfectly integrated into a couple's sex life. It is very exciting to masturbate while watching your partner do it too. The intensity of feelings that show on your partner's face is just great to watch. This has to be introduced into a relationship with care – there must be enough trust and confidence. Masturbation can be a good alternative to sexual intercourse.

Oral Sex

Oral sex is an act whereby the mouth comes into contact with the sexual organs. Many women love to feel the male organ in their hands and suck on it. It is even more exciting for the female to see the male organ shoot out sperm as a reward for their action. This is probably due to the fact that the female orgasm happens from within and does not shoot like the male does... although, I have heard of women who can shoot fluid like men do but I am yet to experience this myself.

Men also enjoy this act since it gives them incredible sensations. The mouth, which feels a lot like the female organ, has an extra gadget – that is the tongue – to cause more stimulation for the male. The tongue is used to create and release tension around the ring of the male organ, while keeping the teeth away from direct contact. Some experts can drive a dick deep into their throats and this can be mind-blowing for the male partner. Men also like to spread the legs of a female partner and suck on their clitoris. A woman's clitoris is a very sensitive point and she enjoys great stimulation when the tongue makes contact with it. The warmth of the mouth when felt in this area causes great stimulation for the female.

Some men also experience great sensations when they taste the juices that the female organs produce. They talk of the juices getting sweeter as the female approaches melting point. With practice, couples easily discover what excites their partners. This type of sex should be approached cautiously since not everyone finds it exciting.

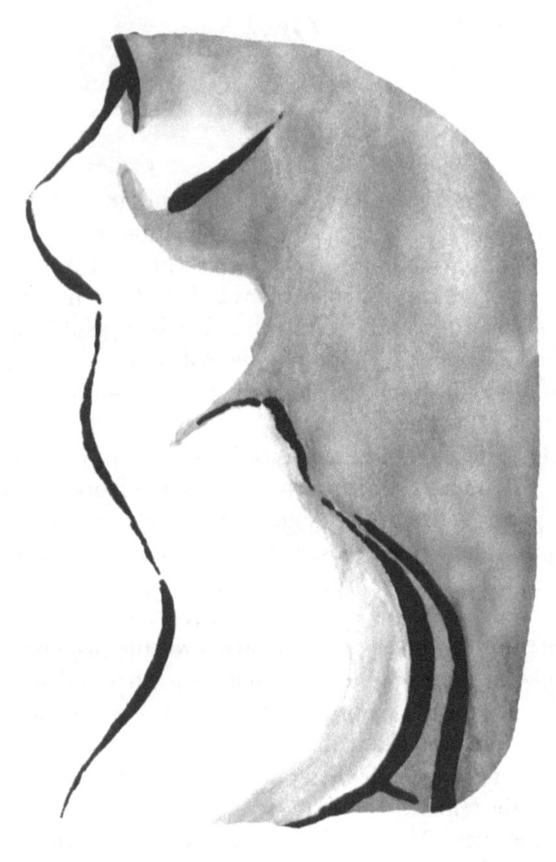

Anal Sex

This is a form of sex where the penis is inserted into the anus of the female partner. Perhaps this type of sex came about from human beings' search for alternative sex.

Some women express a feeling close to being split into two, some others express feeling their insides move. Some describe a sensation of sweet pain. Men equally enjoy anal sex due to the tightness of the anal hole and the visual of the backside of the female.

A couple who have never tried this type of sex ought to approach it with patience and caution. Since the anal opening is smaller than that of the vagina, patience and lubrication is needed for full penetration. The muscles in the area must be relaxed to permit penetration.

The anal area is a very sensitive zone and massaging the area alone can be a great stimulant. The muscles in the area can stretch without pain if the expansion is gradual. I recommend a doggy-style position when doing this for the first time and to constantly keep massaging the vagina and touching the clitoris – this helps the female to relax the muscles in the anus area. I know of females who have experienced multiple orgasms through performing this act. Hygiene plays a major role in this type of act so condoms are recommended for anal penetration.

Fisting

This may sound like a violent kind of sex but it's not. This is a type of sexual act whereby penetration to the vagina is made by the hand. This does not necessarily mean a full fist is inserted as the name implies!

The fingers are moulded and held together, while the hand is gradually inserted into the vagina. Women who have had babies often enjoy this act – I guess the feeling of an outstretched pussy and the feel of the hand reaching the base of the vagina is a great stimulant and often leads to very intense orgasms. Women may find it difficult to talk about this type of sex to their male partners and so may prefer to practise it with other females who share the same feelings. Fear plays a role in this secrecy as they may worry that many men will regard this act as perverse. Men often underestimate the elasticity of the female organ. The fact is, an average vagina can accommodate a penis of practically any size, as well as the body of a baby. The only condition is that the stretch must be gradual. There are inflatable dildos on the market to assist women who want to experience the stretch.

I expect this act to be practised by responsible adults with a good knowledge of what they want but I know of teenage girls who practise this type of sex. Where necessary, a lot of gel must be applied to the hand and vagina. In order to avoid internal cuts from finger nails, thin latex gloves are recommended. Insertion, as well as exiting, must be gradual and internal movement must be gentle.

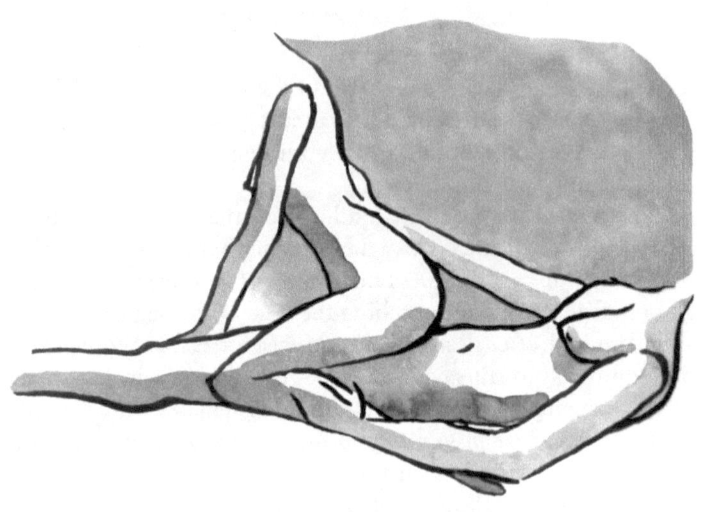

Spanking

This type of act also sounds violent but my experience is that it's not. This is an act whereby the ass of the female is spanked or gradually hit till she reaches orgasm. This can be a great stimulant to the female and a great turn-on for the male. It never stops to amaze me all the things there are to discover about the human body.

This act, just like the previous one, should be initiated with care and patience. The first few strokes to the rear should be gentle and constant since it could be painful. As the ass becomes warm, the skin hardens and a wonder happens – the pain suddenly turns into incredible pleasure and the body seems to want more of it.

I had watched some movies on spanking and this was a big turn-on for me so I brought it up one day with a partner. The female expressed how incredible it felt but did not like the marks it left on her backside. Well, we found out that it was the heat that accumulated on her ass that brought about her orgasm. So I tried rubbing her buttocks with oil and as I kept rubbing at a fast tempo I could feel the heat and suddenly, it happened – she melted like never before! Who knows? You could also discover something great about your partner. Don't be scared to try new things.

The Big Dick

This is undoubtedly one of women's most popular fantasies. Most women like to experience penetration of a huge dick. I guess it is to test their limits or rather to see how much pressure their organs can take. This can be related to a sweet pain effect. Well, if you are a small or medium-sized guy, how do you make your partner live out this kind of fantasy? I guess if you are open enough with your partner you could consider the use of a fairly large dildo to obtain a similar effect without involving outsiders in your sexual affairs. Insertion of a big dildo could be painful if it is done in a rush. Gel must be applied where necessary and patience must be exercised. Men can get very excited watching the penetration and the pleasure the partner derives from it. Again, not all women enjoy this type of act, some women really suffer when their partners are well hung. They would rather have a medium-sized guy. Trust and communication should be the key to unlocking this great fantasy.

Appreciation

It is very important for couples to show appreciation for one another. Humans come in all sizes, shapes and forms – no one is to blame for how they look or how big or small their sex organs are. There is no need to embarrass one's partner for having a small dick, small breasts, big ass, small ass, etc. If you have chosen that partner, why hurt their feelings? Overlooking deficiencies and appreciating one's partner can help bring the best out of that partner. After all, a dick, a pussy, big or small is meant to have the same functions and achieve the same results.

The same applies to breasts and asses. After a good sex act, take time to caress your partner and tell them how good it felt and how much you love and appreciate them rather than making humiliating comments.

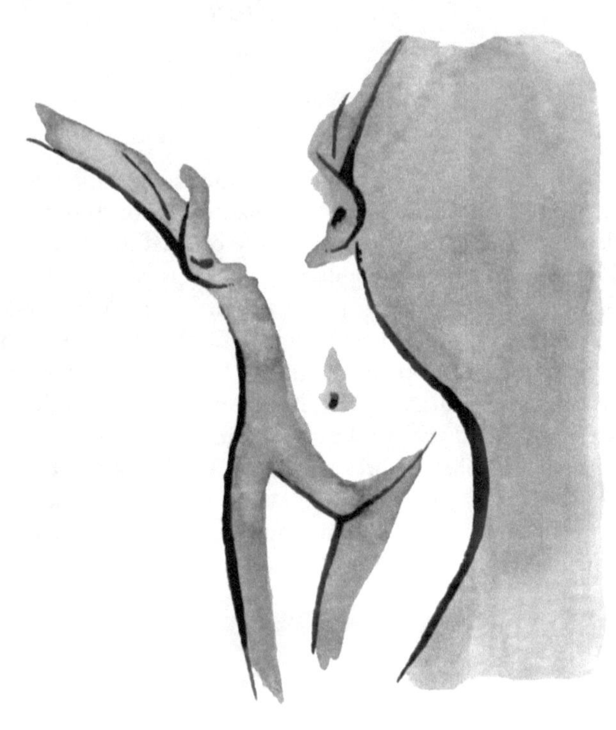

Multiple Orgasms

It is an unforgettable experience for a female to have multiple orgasms. This can be quite demanding on the male if it is all going to be achieved through intercourse. Women need time to reach orgasm, and even more time is needed for multiple orgasms. A man with knowledge of the different ways to make the partner reach orgasm is an ideal lover. After multiple orgasms both partners normally need rest since it can be exhausting.

Choose the right time for it. You may want to organise a sex toolbox for multiple orgasms. The contents may include lubricating gel, different types of dildos, some candles, some ropes, some blindfold scarves, some thin latex gloves, some nipple clippers and anything else you choose to use. The bottom line is to be open and creative and live your fantasy with your partner. Let your partner be the angel, as well as the devil in your life. Let her be the best bitch and the best lover you've ever known. Let him be your playmate and best lover.

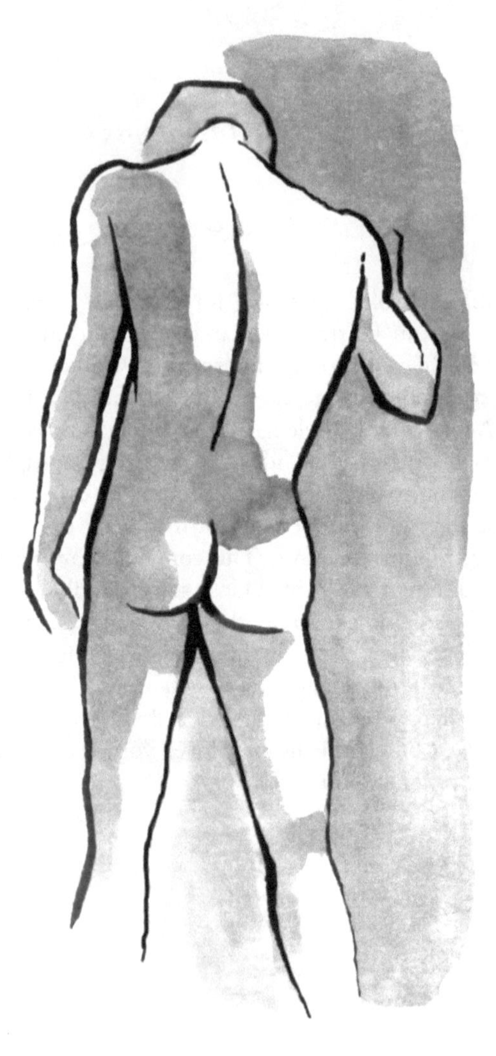

Human Memory

Just like a computer stores things into memory, the human brain also stores sex acts. These can be recalled, replayed and the experiences relived, all in the mind. Most people can replay certain sexual encounters to help them reach climax. Jack could be with Mary, while replaying the encounter with Jill in his mind to reach orgasm…

One can actually see the act as if it were a video playback in the mind. I guess that's where the vocal part of the act becomes crucial. The partner who does not say a word during sex has no audio to the video playback, and that makes this type of video less interesting – it might not keep long in the memory bank. Society has succeeded in making people timid and it takes a lot of effort to overcome this obstacle.

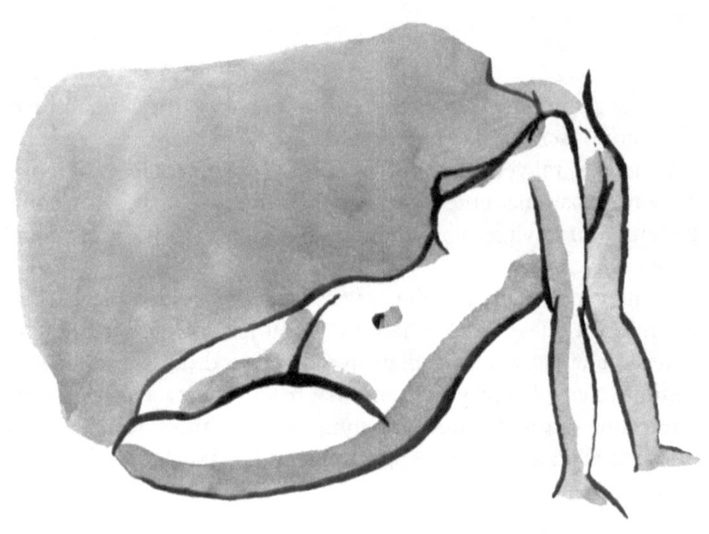

Hygiene

Hygiene plays a vital role in a sexual act. It can be very unpleasant to indulge in sex under unhygienic conditions. It is advisable to wash before indulging in sex. A woman will want to suck on a clean penis rather than a dirty one. A man will want to lick a pussy that smells good. Most men have strong body odour and need to frequently shave and wash. Most of the smells of a man come from armpit sweat, between the legs and residue from bodily functions. Most of the smells on women come from sweat and urine residue that gets caught up in the pubic hair. A shaven pubic area is easier to keep clean than a hairy one. Some men dislike a shaved pussy so it's good to find out your partner's preferences. I cannot overemphasise the need to wash before having sex. Where a whole body wash is not possible, at the least, washing the hands and the sexual organs should be done.

Time

Choosing the right time for a sex act is very crucial in today's pace of living. It has become a common practice to have sex in the night. This can be inconvenient for a partner who is getting up early the next morning. I think time must be taken for sex.

I know of people who don't seem to have enough time for sex and this is a shame. I think having sex daily can be boring and a put-off for one's partner. Choose a time that both partners can enjoy; give your best and have a rest after the act. Occasional quickies might do but time must be taken for a good act. Couples with kids might have to be more careful about the times they choose. Send the kids to the playground, shopping or to school and enjoy without interruption. Couples without kids might enjoy more freedom practicing some of the topics mentioned in this book. Occasional spontaneous acts in the kitchen while making coffee, or in the shower, or on the sofa while watching a movie is always an extra turn-on.

Love Games

I lately came of this idea of love games. I haven't yet tried it but I can imagine how well it could work in an open relationship. It's very simple. Just pick six types of sex activities that are acceptable to you and your partner. Make a list – or sex menu – and number it from 1 to 6. Get a bottle of champagne or wine and when you feel relaxed and in the mood for love, throw a dice to choose from your sex menu. Here is a sample menu:

1. Massage
2. Oral
3. Male Choice
4. Anal
5. Masturbation
6. Female Choice

Note from the Author

While pursuing a career in music, I came into contact with people who were not shy to talk about their sexual experiences. This helped to free me and I started enjoying this gift of nature without reserve. It is now my pleasure to share some of my experiences with the reader. Please consider this a source of information and not porn.

Feel free to live your fantasy and expand on the ideas that I have offered here. I would very much like to hear from you. Any comments, ideas or experiences that you wish to share are very welcome.

sirroto@yahoo.com

RC